THE PAINTER DEPICTED

THIS IS THE THIRTEENTH OF THE
WALTER NEURATH MEMORIAL LECTURES
WHICH ARE GIVEN ANNUALLY EACH SPRING ON
SUBJECTS REFLECTING THE INTERESTS OF
THE FOUNDER
OF THAMES AND HUDSON

THE DIRECTORS WISH TO EXPRESS
PARTICULAR GRATITUDE TO THE GOVERNORS AND
MASTER OF BIRKBECK COLLEGE
UNIVERSITY OF LONDON
FOR THEIR GRACIOUS SPONSORSHIP OF
THESE LECTURES

THE PAINTER DEPICTED

PAINTERS AS A SUBJECT IN PAINTING

MICHAEL LEVEY

THAMES AND HUDSON

First published in the USA in 1982 by
Thames and Hudson Inc., 500 Fifth Avenue,
New York, New York 10110

Library of Congress Catalog Card Number: 81-52700

I have never forgotten how, some twenty years ago, a dull Sunday morning – or should I say simply a Sunday morning? – was enlivened for me by an unexpected telephone call, resulting in my first serious contact with Walter Neurath.

He had some ideas for books. He thought I might be a suitable person to write one of them. He proposed our meeting soon : that very evening at his house. At that date I had so little experience of publishers that I assumed such eagerness and speed must characterize the profession. Now, of course, I realize they characterized the man.

Dropping everything – including a baby – my wife and I hastened that evening to Highgate. Among the ideas exchanged, as four of us strolled after dinner in the darkened garden, was one for a book about the sense of the past as revealed in paintings. This typically appealed to Walter Neurath, as a bold, ranging idea, and though I never wrote that book I remain grateful to him for providing me with other challenges, no less bold and ranging. The theme I touch on in this lecture disinters something of that original project, so I hope it is a not unsuitable tribute to the memory of the founder of Thames and Hudson.

1 NICAISE DE KEYSER (1813–87), *Raphael in his studio*, 1865 (Private Collection)

IN the medium of paint the painter has remarkable opportunities to create works of art whose subject-matter can be the activity of being a painter: in his studio, in private or public life, from birth and childhood to death and posthumous celebration.

Such subject-matter has exercised a great appeal over western European painters from the Middle Ages onwards. The material is almost bewilderingly rich and diverse, even when one excludes, as I largely do, both self-portraits and others. Nor am I attempting here to be comprehensive, or strictly chronological.[1]

Can we sum up the appeal of this subject-matter? Before trying to do so, I think one is bound to notice that it seems more attractive to painters to take painting as their theme than for composers or novelists to treat similarly their respective arts. It is true that, for example, there are operas about the subject of opera; I don't forget in that connection Mozart and Richard Strauss. Gide's *Les Faux-Monnayeurs* is an instance of a novel about a novelist writing a novel: an instance which today may seem a warning against too much ingenuity of that kind in literature. Perhaps it is my own ignorance, but I suspect that examples in music and literature tend to be isolated, atypical, with a somewhat contrived air, when not deliberate *jeux d'esprit*.

In painting, the theme develops, proliferates and by the 19th century is almost absurdly common – sometimes commonplace. Probably most of us tend to recall some garbled scenario, *à la* Max Beerbohm, of Leonardo da Vinci declining to shake hands with Michelangelo, while Raphael and the Fornarina look on. And it might be asked if the theme is worthy of the occasion when we realize that pictures were actually painted with such titles as *Jan Steen sends his son out to trade pictures for beer and wine*, and *Francis Mieris offering his disconsolate wife a portion of the last bottle.*[2]

I shall not claim significance for every picture of this kind executed, yet I feel that many of these prove to have some significance for the painter who did them. Whether the picture is of a studio, a painter at work or on his deathbed, the creator of it expresses tremendous pride in the power of his art – the art of painting. It is a gift, divine or natural. It must be honed by hard work but it deserves – often receives – the world's homage and recognition. The artist is the monarch whom monarchs revere. Art is shown as immortal, though artists die. Because painting is a visual art, everyone may see and appreciate it. Its illusionism can cause astonishment, and before any picture of a painter at work we might pay the tribute paid to Velazquez's *Las Meninas* by Gautier in his quip: 'where is the picture?'

Beyond illusionism there is the inherent pride in the painter's descent from the great painters of the past. And this, I think, is far more than historicism as practised in the historically highly conscious 19th century. Perhaps painters then clung the more desperately to the associations of the great artists of the past through sensing a crisis about the direction of art in their own period. And certainly I believe that personal feelings dictated, more possibly than has always been recognized, choice of subject-matter and treatment, even in those exhibition pictures that so constantly involve the life and death of such famous figures as Raphael, Leonardo and Michelangelo. We may learn nothing – or nothing reliable – about these painters from 19th-century depictions of them, but, rather, something about the painters who chose to depict them.

I think the point can be made by considering two of this type of picture, where the subjects are today far better known than the artists who painted them. Nicaise de Keyser's *Raphael in his studio* looks like an artist's dream of the happy, successful, courted life lived by artists in the Renaissance. In fact, the scenario is drawn directly from Vasari, who tells of Raphael's princely existence; he is shown surrounded by admiring pupils, and what look like several Fornarine, and his contented, popular personality is contrasted with the baleful figure of Michelangelo passing by, excluded and envious. De Keyser might have been surprised to find that posterity had to have his name explained. If not quite a Raphael of his day, he was nevertheless a highly successful

8

2 J.‑A. Garnier (1847‑89), *Le roi s'amuse!* (Leonardo at Fontainebleau), exh. Salon 1874 (Private Collection)

Belgian painter, handsome, popular, receiving many honours, including being honoured by the king.[3] And by putting into his picture Dürer's self‑portrait, following but expanding Vasari's mention that this had been sent to Raphael, he suggests – understandably enough, as he was himself a northern artist – a vision of the Renaissance as not solely an Italian phenomenon.

More unusual in several ways is a picture of nine years later, shown by J.‑A. Garnier at the Salon of 1874, in Paris. It takes the by then well‑established theme of Leonardo and François I, but it does not choose the normal flattering aspect of the French king's honourable treatment of the aged genius. Garnier seems to have been somewhat unconventional, even faintly shocking, in choice of subject‑matter on other occasions.[4] He showed this picture under the sufficiently revealing title *Le roi s'amuse!* And it does convey a strong sense of Leonardo, if not quite mocked as a court jester, at least treated with insulting indifference at the French king's court, bewildered in the midst of alien figures and barely

3 M. GEERAERDTS (1516/21–before 1604), *Miseries of a painter*, 1577
(Bibliothèque Nationale, Paris)

acknowledged by the lounging, womanizing monarch. The picture
could scarcely have been shown during the Second Empire, but the
empire had ceased to be; Napoleon III was exiled and dead; France was
a republic.

Whether or not Garnier intended any criticism of the way the arts
were treated by royalty, his picture is unusual at any time in pointing to
the problems and difficulties of the artist's life. Rarely, if ever, do we find
pictures of painters suffering from difficulties in their art, though there are
compositions which depict the practical difficulties which may face the
artist. It is lack of money, combined with prevalence of family, that
afflicts the painter shown by Geeraerdts. Even he is in his studio, trying
to work.[5]

At work: that is the most sustained aspect of pictures of painters, in
their studios, absorbed by the demands of art. It is already a theme in the

10

4 PICASSO (1881–1973), *Dans l'Atelier*, 10 January 1954

15th century, when the painter is frequently St Luke. It can be seen still providing the inspiration in Picasso's witty and ironic series of drawings of a painter at his easel, himself old while his model is piquantly young and indifferent to him. In one of the most amusing of these more than merely light-hearted compositions, a monkey takes the artist's place at the easel; he does stir the model's interest. At the same time Picasso must have been conscious of the tradition of the *singerie*, where a monkey, ape of nature, is painted as working away in front of an easel. Picasso's variations on famous pictures, including *Las Meninas*, are further evidence of his awareness of art of the past, and there are times when his sense of tradition seems as strong as Reynolds's. He must have spoken for many painters of many periods when he said, 'I have a feeling that Delacroix, Giotto, Tintoretto, El Greco and the rest . . . are all standing behind me watching me at work.'[6]

11

5 VELAZQUEZ (1599–1660), *Las Meninas*, 1656 (Prado, Madrid)

6 VERMEER (1632–75), *A Painter at work, c.* 1665 (Kunsthistorisches Museum, Vienna)

Two paintings are so central to the whole theme that they must be introduced here. They look both backward and forward. They are perhaps the most sheerly sophisticated masterpieces of paintings that take painting as their subject. Each deserves a book in itself, and to be compared and returned to even within the limits here. Velazquez's *Las Meninas* (to continue using this famous but gravely misleading title) and *A Painter at work* by Vermeer must have been painted within a very few years of each other. Variations on the same theme, and united by intense pride in painting as an art of the most artful kind, they stress different aspects.

In *Las Meninas* a modern application is given to the traditional story derived from antiquity, and popular from the Renaissance onwards, of Apelles honoured by Alexander the Great, who visits him in his studio. Also underlying the painting, I believe, is the other association of Apelles with Alexander as the only painter to whom the king would sit. This was to be cited when Titian was honoured by the Emperor Charles V,[7] and it is pertinent in the case of Velazquez, since Philip IV distinguished him in the same way.[8] Both painting as an activity and the painter are honoured in *Las Meninas*, at the centre of which is, however, the king.

In Vermeer's composition, the role of painting is proudly, if tacitly, celebrated. We are shown not the features of the painter but what he is painting: a picture of the Muse of History, whom he will create out of the figure of the girl posing for him. Fame, immortality, can be given by the image no less than by words; the painter serves the ends of history, and perhaps immortalizes himself at the same time.

But it has to be recognized that, for the Middle Ages and the Renaissance, painters and pictures of antiquity survived only in the medium of words. It was not possible to have the same attitude to Apelles or Zeuxis as to the ancient poets, whose works could be read. A few anecdotes and some descriptions of some of their paintings were all that gave body to the names of even the greatest of ancient painters.

There was no Muse of painting. The art lacked altogether any founder-figure, mythical or otherwise, until the emergence of St Luke in the West. There were, in fact, one or two other saints associated with

7 Italian (?) 14th century,
St Luke painting the Virgin

painting, but St Luke was the one who became, in ways still by no means clear, the patron saint of painters.[9] He is − in contrast to the painters of classical antiquity − an *œuvre* in search of a personality. Nothing was known about him, except that traditionally he was supposed to have been a doctor, but already in the 6th century a painting by him, of the Virgin, is mentioned as sent from Jerusalem to Constantinople. Pictures of the Virgin ascribed to him began to be venerated. As late as 1860 Pope Pius IX established a commission to try and settle who painted an image of the Virgin, attributed to St Luke, in the church of S. Maria Maggiore at Rome.[10] Today there is a commission, set up without papal initiative, to try and settle attributions throughout the world to Rembrandt. St Luke as such is not my subject, but he has his relevance; most of the early depictions of painters turn out to be depictions of him.

At first he is shown seated, simply painting away, much as he might be shown writing his gospel, in an unparticularized setting, if there is a setting at all and normally but not always painting an image of the Virgin.[11] The painter is thus shown with no model – not even with a vision to inspire him. He uses his imagination.

By the 15th century, when pictures of St Luke begin to take on new character and variety, painting as an activity could be treated in a secular way, as one of the talents of the children of Mercury. In series of compositions dealing with the qualities and abilities of those born under each planet, the children of Mercury are shown as lively, intelligent and what we would term creative. It is interesting to note in these compositions how in northern Europe painting is conceived of as very much easel painting, whereas in a typical Florentine example it is exterior fresco painting that represents the art. Yet in neither composition is painting treated as anything special; it is simply one among the activities that Mercury inspires.

By the time these prints were produced St Luke was well established north and south of the Alps as the patron of painters, who formed into guilds and confraternities taking his name and introducing him into their statutes.[12] He had become what Cennini calls him: 'primo dipintore cristiano'.[13] It was perhaps for some guild chapel that Rogier

8 (*far left*) German 15th century, *Children of Mercury* (Kupferstichkabinett, Berlin)

9 (*left*) MASTER OF THE PLANETS, *Children of Mercury, c.* 1460–65 (British Museum, London)

10 (*above*) ROGIER VAN DER WEYDEN (*c.* 1399–1464), *St Luke painting the Virgin* (Courtesy, Museum of Fine Arts, Boston, Gift of Mr and Mrs Henry Lee Higginson)

11 NIKLAS MANUEL (1484–1531), *St Luke painting the Virgin* (Kunstmuseum, Bern)

van der Weyden's *St Luke painting the Virgin* was destined. Several things make this picture novel, and not merely the iconography of the saint. His prominence in the composition is remarkable, and he is shown positively studying the Virgin from the life – making a drawing of her that we can presume is preparatory to the portrait he will paint. It is easy to sense an air of scrutiny in the kneeling saint's gaze, as he studies the physical reality before him; what he has drawn is carefully conveyed, and portraiture altogether seems relevant, since it has often been suggested that the features of the saint are the artist's own.[14] They certainly have a strong portrait look to them.

A little more stress is laid on painting as such in a picture which must be broadly indebted to Rogier's, of the same subject and attributed to Bouts (in the Lady Janet Douglas-Pennant Collection). Not only does the interior there seem less heavenly, and more bourgeois, than in Rogier's, but in the small adjoining room there is a hint of a studio, with a painting on an easel. Some other and slightly later depictions of St Luke show the painter at once inspired and overcome by a vision of the Virgin that he has to capture; and Gossaert, who also painted St Luke seated studying a group of the Virgin and Child, shows the saint on his knees and receiving the help of an angel in getting down a record of his vision.[15] Such a vision is largely banished to an upper corner in Niklas Manuel's treatment of the theme. Here the only assistance the painter needs is from a pupil, preparing the surface of a picture in the background; more information is now being given about the painter's contemporary existence, and the final topical touch is that St Luke is a portrait of the artist himself.

Some pictures were painted already in the 15th century dealing with the great painters of antiquity. The story of Zeuxis, who chose a group of girls to inspire him in the task of painting Helen of Troy, was translated into charming contemporary terms by at least one northern artist, illustrating a manuscript of Cicero, where this story is told. The Crotona of the original story has become a Netherlandish town, and Zeuxis is alive and living happily not far from Bruges. Delightful though this depiction is, it illustrates a story as much as do paintings of St Luke. Not, I think, until the following century could a painter and his

12 Netherlandish, late 15th century,
Zeuxis painting girls in his studio: detail
(Bibliotheek der Universiteit,
Ghent)

studio be depicted just as they were, without any religious, classical or planetary overtones.

Agostino Veneziano's print showing the studio, or 'academy' of Bandinelli must be one of the very earliest of such depictions. And it already emphasizes the aspect of study and training – here study by night – which becomes a theme for pictures and prints. Indeed, what we see here is not the actual manual work of the artist so much as the disciplines of application and training which go to make the artist a professional, as well as the lesson inculcated by example, which the master passes on to his pupils. Burgkmair had before this reinterpreted in contemporary, though not merely flattering, terms Alexander's visit to the studio of Apelles in showing the 'Weisskunig', the Emperor Maximilian, in a painter's studio, thus documenting this aspect of the emperor's taste and interest.

Once created, these aspects of depicting the activity of the painter were to develop, especially during the 17th century, with refinements and variations which, however, do not in many cases add significantly to the theme. In Van Haecht's picture of Alexander visiting Apelles, the

13 AGOSTINO VENEZIANO (1490–1540), *Bandinelli's Academy in Rome*, 1531
(British Museum, London)

novelty is in the setting: a picture gallery rather than a studio. This type
of picture becomes a subject in its own right, quite often with
contemporary visitors, royal patrons or collectors.[16] The paintings
shown in Van Haecht's composition are themselves topical; many of
them at the time were in Cornelis van der Geest's collection at
Antwerp, whose keeper or curator was Van Haecht. As for the aspect of
the artist working with his pupils, this was a popular subject for
drawings in the circle of Rembrandt, sometimes with a touch or so of
humour in the variety of pupil, aged and young, studying the model
along with the master himself.

14 H. Burgkmair (1473–1531), *The Emperor Maximilian in a painter's studio, c.* 1518

In Molenaer's picture of an artist's studio we see the figures who are his models both naturally, as they amuse themselves in the studio, and as composed by the artist into the painting on his easel. This is a rare example, though not unique, where the painter shows us 'life', as it were, and also the art he makes from it, by allowing us to see the picture that results. Another concept of the studio appears in Mazo's re-working, downgrading (at Vienna), of his father-in-law's *Las Meninas*. Instead of the royal family, we confront the painter's own family. They occupy the foreground, and the painter and his easel disappear into the distance. The king is no longer signalled as present though outside the composition, as in *Las Meninas*, but is there only in the effigy on the easel. Almost by accident, perhaps, Mazo has invented another type of picture: the artist's studio is filled with his friends and family. Pictures of this kind were to become very popular in the early 19th century.[17]

An emphasis on the training of the artist led to pictures of the young artist, the pupil shown without a master but training himself, studying in preparation for his future career. One may think first of Chardin and other painters of this period in France, but it was in the 17th century that the theme developed and was disseminated through engravings. Vaillant's composition is characteristic, and although often catalogued as a picture of a boy drawing, it is in fact of a boy reading or at least studying a book.[18] The inspiration of the art of the past which he will copy, or has already copied, is made patent by the cast of the Christ Child from Michelangelo's group at Bruges; and there may be some

15 W. VAN HAECHT (1593–1637), *Alexander in Apelles' studio* (Bestegui Collection, Paris)

16 REMBRANDT follower 17th century, *Rembrandt's studio* (Staatliche
Kunstsammlungen, Weimar)

17 J. M. MOLENAER (*c.* 1609/10–68), *Painter's studio*, 1631 (Staatliche Museen, Berlin)

18 Attributed to W. VAILLANT
(1623–77), *A young artist*
(National Gallery, London)

19 (*right*) SAMUEL VAN
HOOGSTRATEN (1627–78),
Amoris Caufa: detail of peep-show
exterior, 1654–62 (National
Gallery, London)

association to be felt between the boy in reality and the sculpted, divine
Boy. Even when the theme of practising art was shown in a domestic
context, treated partly as genre, by, for example, Metsu (in a picture in the
National Gallery), there is detectable about the woman artist a sense of
serious concentration; she may be an amateur, at work in her own home,
but her attitude is fully professional.

All these examples precede Vermeer's painting of a painter at work.
And almost certainly this is true of another work of art which, I think,
has its relevance for the Vermeer, though not previously related to it.
This is the peep-show box by Samuel van Hoogstraten (in the National
Gallery), probably painted in the late 1650s.[19] Here, we are concerned
with the least regarded aspect of this fascinating object, its exterior. No
doubt the whole box is meant to form a demonstration of the ingenuity of

art, and certainly Art is the theme of the rather poor, and damaged, scenes on the outside. These are based on some sentences in Cicero's *De beneficiis* referring to the incentives for the painter. He may be urged on by thoughts of glory, and though it is not clear what he is painting he is having a gold chain put round his neck by a putto who also crowns him with a laurel wreath, one of Clio's attributes. Pointedly different is the degrading influence of money; Hoogstraten illustrates that by a painter who is painting a portrait, a comparatively low form of art. Most interesting of all for my theme is the third scene, showing an artist making a drawing of the Muse Urania. There are few or no other pictures of this subject – painters depicting any of the Muses – which, in Hoogstraten's case, serves to illustrate sheer love of his art as the artist's inspiration. When, several years later, Hoogstraten published his

20 J. B. WEENIX (1621–60?), *Antony and Cleopatra*:
costume detail, *c.* 1660 (National Gallery, London)

Inleyding tot de Hooge Schoole der Schilderkonst (1678), he dedicated each
part to one of the nine Muses, the last part being dedicated to Urania,
Muse of Astronomy, as symbolizing the artist's aspiration towards the
sublime. On the outside of the peep-show he seems to suggest that the
painter is in the Muse's service; it is she herself who poses for him. In the
Vermeer it may be rather that the Muse (i.e. history) needs the services of
the painter, and of course a girl models the Muse for him. At the same
time there are perhaps hints also in the picture of Hoogstraten's line of
thought, not least in the artist seeking glory – a perfectly honourable end,
mingled with love of his art.

As for the identity of the artist in Vermeer's composition, it has
recently become customary to assume not only that he is not Vermeer but

that the costume he wears is deliberately archaic, 'Burgundian 15th century',[20] for reasons that do not seem entirely clear. It would be odd to set such a figure in what is patently an interior in 17th-century Holland, if not indeed specifically in Delft. And parallels for the costume can be found in some other Dutch 17th-century pictures, as for example one by Weenix of very much the same date.[21] It seems far more likely that the costume is fashionable, if slightly fancy, and that the painter wears it as another indication of the status of his art. It brings to mind Leonardo's observation in the *Trattato della Pittura* about how the painter – as opposed to the sculptor – sits at his easel relaxed and well dressed.[22] The *Trattato* was published in a French translation in 1651 and might, therefore, have been known to Vermeer; even if he never read it, he might have taken an interest in anything which spoke of the painter's status, since he himself was a *hoofdman* at thirty of the Guild of St Luke in Delft, about the date probably that he painted this picture. It is no doubt concerned with 'the painter,' not an individual as such, but between that image and Vermeer there cannot have been great distinction. No one can prove the identity of the painter depicted – Vermeer has seen to that – yet an element of self-identification would seem unavoidable. In reaction against too simple earlier interpretations of the scene as Vermeer's studio, modern scholarship is in danger perhaps of missing something obvious and intentional.

At least there can be no problem over the identity of the painter in *Las Meninas*. It is the picture he is working on that has caused discussion. Again, proof will never be forthcoming but since the final canvas itself is a group of his family, and his court, including his court painter, assembled under his own gaze, with Philip IV taking his place within as well as without the composition, it seems most likely that Velazquez is painting exactly the picture, *Las Meninas*, that hangs today in the Prado.[23]

Both this picture and that by Vermeer look forward; they culminate in the 19th century with, most obviously, Courbet's *L'Atelier* and the more sympathetic *A studio in the Batignolles* by Fantin-Latour, which pays homage to Manet, while Courbet characteristically pays homage to himself. In Courbet's huge composition, the various levels of the world,

21 G. COURBET (1819–72), *L'Atelier*: detail, 1855 (Louvre, Paris)

22 H. Fantin-Latour (1836–1904), *A studio in the Batignolles*, 1870 (Louvre, Paris)

as it were, invade the artist's studio; he takes on a sort of cosmic significance, the hero, if not virtually the god, in a secular apotheosis. There is nothing grandiose about the scene in Manet's studio, where, however, a figure of Athena, goddess of the arts, presides over the group gathered there.[24] This is no visit by a patron to the painter. About him stand his friends, several of them painters; in the foreground is a fairly new figure in artistic affairs, the critic, in this case Astruc, himself also a sculptor. We do not see what Manet is painting but very probably it is Astruc's portrait.

These pictures have a good deal to say about the status of the artist as artists see it. They are also concerned to record factually the appearance of the painter: to convey personality and something of his environment. In their way, they are history pictures, though their subjects happen to be

29

23 Attributed to UCCELLO (*c.* 1397–1475), *Famous Florentine Artists* (Louvre, Paris)

painters, and living ones at that. And there, too, they come at the end of a
tradition.

It is not surprising that it is to Florence that one must turn for the
earliest examples of painted records of painters' appearances. One of the
first of these to survive may well be of about the same date as Rogier van
der Weyden's *St Luke.* As that possibly was, it may have been destined
to decorate a guild of St Luke building, though in this case a secular
room. Associated more or less with Uccello, the panel would seem to
group a number of famous but not strictly contemporary artists.[25] Their
exact identities are the subject of debate, but to Vasari, at least, the left-
hand figure represented Giotto, and he based his portrait of Giotto in the
1568 edition of the *Vite* on it. Giotto was certainly the first Western
painter whose features were to be recreated, if not preserved, in paintings
and in sculpture. The 15th-century, essentially Florentine, panel of

24 Attributed to F. SALVIATI (1510–63), *Famous Italian Artists* (Fitzwilliam Museum,
Cambridge)

25 G. VASARI (1511–74),
*Duke Cosimo I and artists of
his day*, 1556–62
(Palazzo Vecchio, Florence)

famous artists was to be revised in the following century, now quite
consciously crossing barriers of chronology, when it was copied with
substitution of the 'modern' figures of Raphael and Michelangelo.[26]

Vasari's writings about the artists of the past are in themselves tribute
to a new sense of history, and it is right that he should be involved in
doing something similar in pictorial terms.[27] His work in the Palazzo
Vecchio at Florence gave him opportunities, in dealing with scenes from
the lives of members of the Medici family, to touch on their artistic
interests. Thus Cosimo, *Pater patriae*, was shown directing the building
of the church of S. Lorenzo, though inevitably Brunelleschi appeared in
the same composition. And this tradition was to be echoed in depicting
Duke Cosimo, Vasari's patron, who is shown seated, and in
contemporary dress, amid the artists of his day. They are not so
prominent as their patron, at best planets revolving around him as the

sun and centre of their lives. And that was less flattery than the uncomfortable truth. On the other hand, the Duke is probably the first princely patron to be shown in this way, surrounded by artists.

Not very far away, in the Santa Croce district, Vasari had his own house and the freedom to decorate it as he chose.[28] Here he turned for subject-matter to the painters of antiquity; in the *Vite* he began with a sketch of the history of painting, which found space for Apelles, 'so highly esteemed and honoured . . . by Alexander the Great', before he settled down to modern times with the birth of Cimabue in Florence, and to shed the first light on the art of painting. He frescoed Apelles, working away by night at his picture of Diana, using a variety of female models, and possibly he thought of himself, 'highly esteemed' by Duke

26 G. VASARI
Apelles painting Diana
(Casa Vasari, Florence)

Cosimo. He framed the antique subject-matter round with a frieze that depicted in medallions great Italian artists of recent times, as well as the Medici arms. And the final context must have been given by his own presence, making, as it were, a living link in the chain that went back to Apelles.

Vasari was always in the service of someone or something. A notable opportunity came in 1564, with the death of Michelangelo, for him to serve both his Duke and the cause of art. The ceremonies which were held in Florence to commemorate Michelangelo were unprecedented.[29] Nowhere had an artist's death been the subject of such public and pageant-like mourning, and Vasari was at the core of the discussions and arrangements. Catafalques and funeral decorations were nothing new, but art had not previously been enlisted to commemorate an artist.

The greatest novelty lay in commemorating the artist with large-scale paintings, covering the most famous or significant moments in his long career. Though the pictures are lost, descriptions of them and some drawings survive. Homage by the reigning family of Medici to the great artist was one aspect, utilizing actual events such as the young Prince Francesco getting up from his chair and seating Michelangelo in it, and, even more striking, an occurrence when the Duke himself met Michelangelo in Rome and treated him with such respect that he had the artist sitting in a chair beside him. Neither Vasari nor Cellini, one may assume, was ever received by the Duke in that way.

Another of the compositions provided the germ for those paintings, especially popular in the 19th century, of the first steps of the young genius. It showed the boy Michelangelo received by Lorenzo de'Medici in the sculpture garden at S. Marco; this is more than a piece of Medici propaganda, for it illustrates the natural bent of artistic genius, something Vasari stresses in telling how the youthful Giotto was discovered by Cimabue: the child who is naturally gifted will manifest that gift even when brought up in the wild. The subject of Giotto discovered was to be quite popular with 19th-century painters; and as well as the young Raphael, inevitably, there are pictures of the young Titian, the Bellini boys and, less expectedly, the young Benjamin West.[30]

27 Florentine, 16th century, *Duke Cosimo I and Michelangelo*: detail (Museum of Fine Arts, Budapest)

28 Florentine, 16th century, *Michelangelo as a boy in the garden of S. Marco*: detail (Gabinetto Disegni e Stampe, Uffizi, Florence)

29 FEDERICO ZUCCARO (*c.* 1540/3–1609), *Michelangelo watching Taddeo Zuccaro at work*: detail (Albertina, Vienna)

The basic concept behind the Michelangelo series is of genius early recognized, honoured by the world and triumphant in death. Michelangelo thus appeared not only in the company of princes and popes but in the Elysian Fields, accompanied by an assembly of artists ranging from Zeuxis to Pontormo, and including Masaccio and Uccello. We may be reminded of the late 18th- and 19th-century assemblies of this kind, and it was especially noted of the Michelangelo composition that the 'invention' was quite poetical and also 'new'.[31] Comparable pictures, dealing with events in Titian's life, were planned

36

in Venice for his grand funeral, a few years later, which did not take place.[32] Michelangelo was the first artist to be revived to play a part in other pictures on other themes. He was included by Vasari among the representatives of Florence in a picture painted to greet Joanna of Austria when she entered the city in 1565.[33] And when Federico Zuccaro designed a series of compositions commemorating his brother Taddeo, who had died prematurely at thirty-seven, the same age as Raphael, he depicted Michelangelo watching Taddeo at work frescoing the Palazzo Mattei at Rome. In the following century, Michelangelo's great-nephew commissioned the series of pictures in the Casa Buonarotti, taking up and giving firmer expression to the subjects that had been treated at Michelangelo's funeral ceremonies, and including some new ones.

By that time, however, Raphael's reputation probably stood higher generally. He had been the subject of a still rather baffling picture, presumably 16th-century work, which while paying him homage

30 N. FERRUCCI (1574–1650), *Michelangelo and artists of his day* (Casa Buonarotti, Florence)

31 Style of RAPHAEL, 16th century, *Raphael watching St Luke painting* (Accademia di S. Luca, Roma)

faintly suggests that he needed the intervention of St Luke to help him paint the Madonna and Child. Among the compositions that pay homage to his image, literally, during the 17th century there is that of Maratti, expressing no doubt a personal tribute.[34] Title-pages were to borrow what is very much the imagery of tombs. Here Fame trumpets the immortal nature of Raphael's art, and the Arts deplore the mortal nature of the man. This type of composition was to become very popular, with a change of likeness for the artist concerned. More interesting, as more truly a 'history' picture involving a painter, is Maratti's composition of Annibale Carracci raising the fallen art of Painting. It is true that this is partly an allegory but Annibale himself is carefully shown as a lifelike figure, in action, and a recognizable portrait.[35]

These are all examples of homage to artists of the same nationality as the devisers. Perhaps the most striking aspect of Giordano's large-scale picture of *Rubens painting an allegory of Peace* is that it pays homage to a

32 J. J. DE RUBEIS (after C. Maratti), *Homage to Raphael*. Title page of *Imagines Veteris ac Novi Testamenti . . .*, Rome 1675

33 P. AQUILA (after C. Maratti), *Annibale Carracci raises Painting*: detail. Title-page of *Galeriae Farnesianae Icones*, Rome 1663

foreign painter – and in that it may well be the first picture of its kind.
Little is known about this picture's history or how it came to be
commissioned. It is hard to believe that it represents merely a personal
tribute from Giordano to Rubens. It might have been commissioned in
Naples by a Spanish patron, and it seems to have some references beyond
painting. Rubens may be seen as someone whose concern for peace in
Europe extended to doing more than just paint allegories of it. Renewed
peace in Europe may have prompted the picture in the first place.
Assuming a suggested stylistic dating of the 1660s, there could be some
reference to the Peace of Aix-la-Chapelle in 1668, a peace by which
Spain gained and France was curbed.

Rubens was soon to become a familiar subject for painted tributes,[36]
notably French ones. Charles de la Fosse executed three pictures for his
patron Crozat, each a homage to a painter esteemed by them both:

34 (*left*) L. GIORDANO
(1634–1705), *Rubens painting*
an allegory of Peace (Prado,
Madrid)

35 French (?), ? 18th century,
Homage to Rubens (Graves
Art Gallery, Sheffield)

Titian, Correggio and Rubens. The pictures are lost, but the one
dealing with Correggio is recorded as showing 'Nature, surrounded by
the Graces', presiding over his birth.[37] The exact subject of the Rubens
seems unclear, but a print which exists may echo the composition.[38]
Somewhat similar is a painting, presumably French and from around
1700, which may have been prepared for some title-page of a book of
Rubens's work; the artist remains part of a decorative–allegorical
framework, of a kind that would soon become considered rather old-
fashioned.

Already in one of the compositions serving as a frontispiece to the
Œuvre gravé of Watteau, published by Jullienne, the painter and his
patron are seen side by side, uniting two arts in a natural woodland
setting. Although attributed to Watteau himself, this composition has the
air of having been put together for the purpose of the volume; in any

41

36 N. H. TARDIEU (after
Watteau?), *Watteau and Jean
de Jullienne*: detail.
Frontispiece to the *Œuvre
gravé de Watteau*, 1731

case, it disseminates more than just a portrait of the dead artist, creating
around him a climate that is almost romantically Watteauesque.

Another French title-page, of not very much later, introduces the type
of composition more usually associated with the end of the century.[39]
For his own translation of the *Dialogo della Pittura* of Lodovico Dolce,
Vleughels designed a scene of Michelangelo and Vasari visiting Titian
in Rome when he was painting his *Danaë*. This might indeed be
subtitled in 19th-century style: 'Michelangelo starts back in shock on
first seeing one of Titian's pictures'. Since the *Dialogo* is much concerned
with the superior merits of Raphael, Vleughels had the not altogether
happy thought of introducing him in the shape of a faintly smirking
bust, supposedly part of the décor in Titian's Roman studio. The result
is a composition which has the novelty of bringing together a trio not
otherwise likely to be found juxtaposed.

42

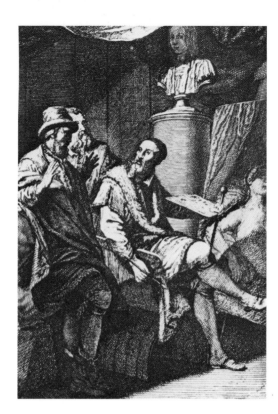

37 N. Vleughels
(1668–1737), *Michelangelo
visiting Titian*

A further and more serious indication of the quite early development
in 18th-century France of subject-matter normally thought of as
appearing much later is a painting unfortunately lost but recorded as
painted and exhibited by Charles Eisen in 1752.[40] In that year he
showed at the Académie de Saint-Luc a picture derived in subject from
Vasari, via de Piles, of *Signorelli painting his dead son*. This stoic theme,
where the emotions of the father and the artist compete, is a remarkable
anticipation of the themes typical of David and other painters twenty or
thirty years later. On the face of Signorelli was, it is noted, a mixture of
sorrow and strength, and that, too, suggests the later climate of the
period. Nothing comparable was to be exhibited for many years at the
Salon, and perhaps Eisen consciously chose a dramatic, poignant
subject concerning a painter since he was exhibiting at the painters'
own, somewhat less established and esteemed, academy. The subject

43

38 MANUEL DE LA CRUZ (1750–92), *Deathbed of Mengs, c.* 1779 (Prado, Madrid)

44

39 J. STOLCKER (1724–85),
Rembrandt in his studio
(British Museum, London)

itself was to remain a rare one, even when the fashion for affecting themes of this kind developed; and the only other painter who seems to have chosen it is Dyce in the 19th century.[41]

In the course of the 18th century great artists died, among them Boucher and Tiepolo and Gainsborough. None of them received any special homage at death. That was reserved for the artist who was probably one of the most respected names in Europe: Mengs. He died in Rome in 1779, and the scene of his deathbed by Manuel de la Cruz probably dates from not very long afterwards.[42] Although only a drawing, it was possibly intended to be engraved or even perhaps made into a painting. Spain prominently mourns the artist, whose picture is being completed by the Graces, while the dying Mengs is sustained by Painting and crowned with the laurel of immortality by Fortune.

The deathbed of artists was soon to be a popular and familiar subject in pictures, but not every painter had to be revived only as a corpse.

45

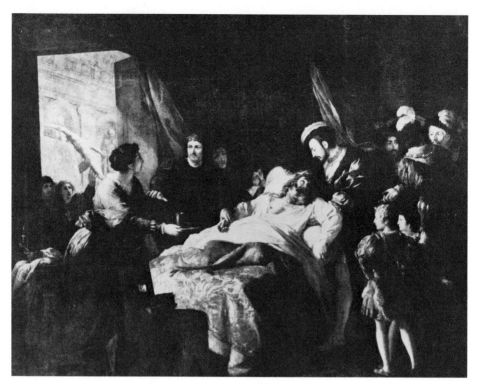

40 F. G. MÉNAGEOT (1774-1816), *Death of Leonardo da Vinci*, exh. Salon 1781 (Musée de l'Hotel de Ville, Amboise)

Rembrandt, not yet canonized by 19th-century faith, appeared quite cheerfully, an almost bustling, busy figure in his studio, a subject for neither woe nor awe.[43]

Not Rembrandt but Leonardo da Vinci was the painter who, for some reason, became the first subject for deathbed portrayal, where artists of the past were concerned. The subject derives from Vasari's account of how Leonardo had the honour to die in the arms of François I, the king of France. The theme is thus less pathetic than glorious. It takes a post-antique artist a step beyond Apelles singled out by Alexander and is the final homage that a ruler can pay to a painter. It may also hint at how the modern monarch should treat the painters of his own day.

Aptly, it might seem, Ménageot's picture of this subject, exhibited at the Salon in 1781, was an official, virtually royal, commission.[44] But it was not the first treatment of the subject; Angelica Kauffmann had exhibited a picture of it at the Royal Academy in 1778. It was drawn at some date by Cosway[45] and was to be taken as a subject by Singleton at the very end of the century. In Ménageot's picture the subject is explicable not so much in terms of an interest in the painter, Leonardo, as in an incident of French history and the uplifting behaviour of a French monarch.

While it heralds a taste for deathbeds, including the deathbeds of artists,[46] it also announces a concern for history, in the sense of reviving or creating awareness of the past, often in national terms. It meant also a respect for the past which helped foster the growth of public museums.[47] What the arts had achieved was, naturally enough, to be the subject frequently of decoration in those institutions, and allied ones. What had been a new concept at the time of Michelangelo's death — to show him mingling with other artists in the Elysian Fields — becomes quite a commonplace in the Elysiums and pantheons of the 19th century, typified by Delaroche's hemicycle in the Ecole des Beaux-Arts in Paris, but initiated by the *Elysium* of Barry in the Royal Society of Arts, executed in 1780.

Yet these assemblages of great figures of the past are inevitably static and undramatic. They represent ideal history, under an eternal gaze, rather than bringing to life the human stories of individual artists: how they lived and were honoured, and of course how they died. These were topics which Vasari had written about with no less interest than he wrote about their art. Literature was bound to be the source of many of the incidents that came to be painted; it recorded often the interesting human detail that would help to make vivid the painter not as artist but as man. And this making vivid is consciously addressed to the new audience, created by public exhibitions, who may be indifferent to style or even quality in a picture but can respond to what is depicted, especially in straightforward human terms. Whether aware of doing so or not, the painter of such pictures is making a plea for a better understanding of painters in general, as well as the art of painting. Perhaps art must remain a mystery, but at least the public can be affected by seeing depicted the last interview of Reynolds and Gainsborough (a

41 A. ANSIAUX (1764–1840), *Poussin introduced by Richelieu to Louis XIII*, 1817 (Musée des Beaux-Arts, Bordeaux)

genuinely moving subject),[48] Lippo Lippi falling in love with the nun[49] and the madness of Hugo van der Goes,[50] and thus sense the man behind the genius. When shown at work, the painter tends still to be seen in strongly human terms. His subject is often enough before him, whether found in a natural, outdoor state, or in the studio: whether it is Willem van de Velde in a boat[51] or the Fornarina sitting on Raphael's lap.

By the 19th century, the possibilities for subject-matter are endless. It would be far easier to make a list of those painters who were not depicted than of those who were; what seems striking in this connection is that the painters usually thought of as rediscovered during that century tend not to be popular as subjects for pictures.[52] Few or no pictures feature

48

42 P. N. BERGERET (1782–1863), *Charles V and Titian*, exh. Salon 1808 (Musée des Beaux-Arts, Bordeaux)

Botticelli, Piero della Francesca, Ghirlandaio and so on; Fra Angelico is not common, nor is Jan van Eyck.

At the same time, certain themes return or develop. Perhaps the most obvious is that of Alexander and Apelles, interpreted in terms of European painters and their sovereigns, continuing more fancifully what is expressed factually in *Las Meninas*. The royal visit to the painter, or the latter's introduction to royalty, can be illustrated by examples from all the major national schools and often blends with national patriotism. At the Salon of 1817, after the restoration of the Bourbons, Ansiaux exhibited his picture of *Poussin introduced by Richelieu to Louis XIII*.[53] Some years earlier Bergeret had painted the familiar anecdote of the Emperor Charles V picking up the brush of Titian, and that story

49

43 H. J. Scholten (1824–1907), *Princess of Orange in Van der Helst's studio,*
c. 1860 (Rijksmuseum, Amsterdam)

might come to a painter's mind, as it did to Lawrence in reality[54] when
an emperor helped him with the pegs of his easel. An oddity of Bergeret's
picture is that Charles V looks very like François I. In Germany the
theme might be illustrated by the Emperor Maximilian sitting to
Dürer.[55] In Holland it was, for example, the studio of Van der Helst
that is visited by royalty, in this case the Princess of Orange. In Belgium
de Keyser painted the visit of Margaret of Austria to Memling.[56] In
England the two most popular monarchs for treatment in this context
were Henry VIII and of course Charles I, though at least one picture
was painted of Philip IV knighting Velazquez.[57] An Italian picture of
Maria de' Medici visiting Ruben's studio is possibly to be explained in terms of the patron's nationality rather than the painter's.[58]

44 E. M. WARD (1816–79), *Hogarth's studio*: detail, exh. RA 1863 (City Art Gallery, York)

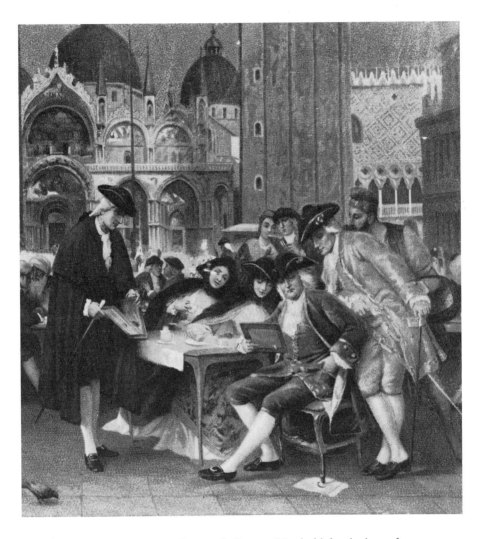

45 (*above left*) After A. EBERLE (1804–32), *Dürer and Raphael before the throne of Art*: detail

46 (*left*) H. LEYS (1815–69), *Frans Floris going to a feast*, 1853 (Wallace Collection, London)

47 (*above*) G. BERTINI (1825–98), *Guardi selling his pictures on the Piazza*: detail (Moro, Rome)

48 W. DYCE (1806–64), *Titian's first essay in colouring*, exh. RA 1857 (Art Gallery and Museum, Aberdeen)

49 E. FÖRSTER (1800–85), *Cimabue discovering the young Giotto, c.* 1833 (Kunstmuseum, Düsseldorf)

The basic message of all these examples is the homage that rank pays, or should pay, to genius. A masterpiece should excite awe, even if this is of a naive kind, as is suggested in E. M. Ward's picture of Hogarth's studio, with his portrait of Captain Coram being looked at by the foundlings and others, while the sitter and painter hide behind it, listening to the comments. The choice of Hogarth for the subject is very much a national one; it conveys a pride in a painter who was probably not the subject of pictures outside England. It was in Germany, not Italy, that compositions were produced showing Dürer and Raphael meeting as equals, sometimes shaking hands like rival football managers and bringing in their trains such subordinate figures as the pope and the emperor. Even more frankly local is the choice of Frans Floris as the subject for a painting by his fellow-citizen, Baron Leys, himself the pride of 19th-century Antwerp.[59] And Floris is shown as very much a gentlemanly figure, going in style to a painters' feast of a splendid civic kind that suggests the status held by artists there. More of a criticism is suggested by a very rare depiction of Guardi, selling his pictures, or trying to, in the Piazza at Venice.[60] That subject was unlikely to be painted by anyone other than an Italian.

As well as touching on the status of the painter as a general topic, many of the subjects chosen have a direct personal application for the painters selecting them. It is not always a matter merely of a striking anecdote for its own sake. This seems especially true of some pictures which deal with the childhood of the painter, going back as a theme once again to the pictures for Michelangelo's funeral. The incident behind Förster's *Cimabue discovering the young Giotto* is the story told by Vasari, as the painter/art historian would very well know. But it has been suggested that there is a personal application, since Förster had been very much the protégé of a great figure of an earlier generation, Peter Cornelius.[61] Without claiming to be another Giotto, Förster may well be expressing something of the debt he felt towards his teacher. The opposite childhood experience, impelled by natural talent, but undiscovered and alone, is conveyed in equally personal terms, I believe, in Dyce's *Titian's first essay in colouring*, a subject which has often seemed an odd one for such a strongly linear, sub-Nazarene painter to choose.

50 J. A. D. INGRES (1780–1867), *Raphael and the Fornarina*, 1814 (Courtesy of the Fogg
Art Museum, Harvard University, Bequest Grenville L. Winthrop)

51 J. M. W. TURNER (1775–1851),
*Rome from the Vatican: Raphael and
the Fornarina*: detail, 1819–20
(Tate Gallery, London)

52 J. M. W. TURNER
Canaletto painting Venice: detail,
exh. RA 1833 (Tate Gallery, London)

Dyce has certainly missed or obscured the point of the original anecdote, told by Ridolfi, about how Titian as a boy created his earliest painting out of flower dyes. The introduction of a statue of the Virgin (Titian's subject for his painting) might suggest that Titian is going to colour this, whereas he has studied it in a drawing. However, the significance lies elsewhere. It was Titian's first 'essay' that showed his father that he was gifted, and as a result he took him down to Venice and apprenticed him as a painter. When we turn to the biography of Dyce, we find that not only was he a self-taught painter, but he found it necessary to convince his father of his talent, and in fact painted a picture which had this effect.[62]

Personal sympathy helps to explain how the attraction for Ingres of Raphael, beginning as artistic homage, deepened into emotional identification at the time of his marriage to Madeleine Chapelle.[63] The cycle he had planned on the life of Raphael became instead several depictions of Raphael and the Fornarina, showing the artist's love as the inspiration of his work, secular and religious. How personal is Ingres's response is emphasized by another treatment of Raphael and the Fornarina, of only a few years later, by Turner. He exhibited it in 1820, the three hundredth anniversary of Raphael's death, but it documents the impact on him of Rome, seen for the first time in the previous year.[64] His Raphael seems dreaming more about his art than about his mistress, and his pictures include not only the familiar *Madonna della Sedia* once again but an improbable proto-Claudian landscape which might stand for the type of picture Turner wished Raphael had painted; Turner has painted it for him.

A similar sympathy must lie behind Turner's painting of Canaletto at work in Venice[65] – the only picture probably of this artist. For Turner, Canaletto takes his inspiration from the given spot; he responds to nature in the very way that Ruskin would deny, and around him Turner makes rise a city at once more magical and more jumbled in its boats, sails and posts (almost dwarfing the painter as he works) than it appears in any picture by Canaletto himself. The homage is as much to Venice as to Canaletto; in later paintings Turner would dispense with the painter and depict simply the city.

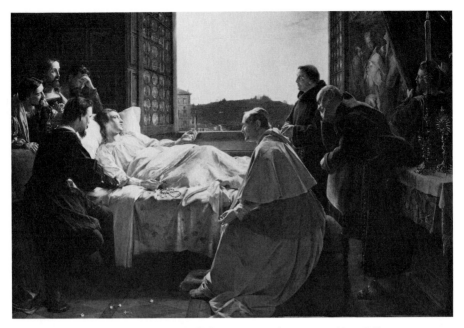

53 H. N. O'NEIL (1817–80), *Raphael's last moments*, exh. RA 1866 (Art Gallery, Bristol)

Finally, there is the sheerly human aspect of the artist's life, conveyed sometimes in the conflict between the human being and his role as artist,[66] which Eisen had illustrated. Most poignant of all must the premature death of the artist himself. Raphael had been the subject for plenty of pictures showing him mourned at death, but it is the actual moment of his dying that is shown by O'Neil (in a picture exhibited at the Royal Academy in 1866),[67] trying to convey the artist's farewell to the world, as he turns to cast a last look over Rome, while his final picture, *The Transfiguration*, is unveiled at the end of his bed. Eisen's theme is given additional pathos in the subject of Tintoretto painting his dead daughter, which was to be depicted in both France and England. This deals not only with the father who paints his child but, since Marietta Tintoretto was a painter, is also a lament for the prematurely dead artist. What the great artist suffers in human terms takes on the

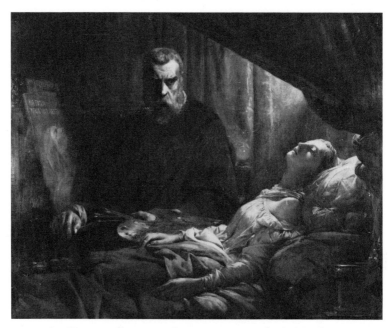

54 L. COGNIET (1794–1880), *Tintoretto painting his dead daughter*, 1845
(Musée des Beaux-Arts, Bordeaux)

more resonance from his stature. Michelangelo, as the supreme example of the giant, frightening, yet lonely figure, is made sympathetic by being depicted caring for his sick servant[68] or, in a memorable example by a painter little-known today, kissing the hands of the corpse of Vittoria Colonna. Fully to appreciate this, the spectator needs to know the incident as described by Condivi; Michelangelo always regretted that at the moment of bending over the body he had not kissed her face.

Even pictures which at first glance appear too trivial for discussion may turn out to have some meaning for those who painted them. *Angelica Kauffmann visiting Reynolds' studio*, shown at the Royal Academy in 1892, would now hardly detain anyone, except that the choice of subject makes sense when we understand that the painter was a woman, Margaret Dicksee, daughter and sister of painters. She might well give glamour to the scene of the first president of the Academy receiving a

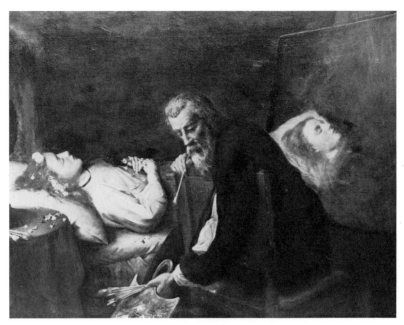

55 H. N. O'NEIL, *Tintoretto painting his dead daughter,* exh. RA 1873
(Wolverhampton Art Gallery and Museum)

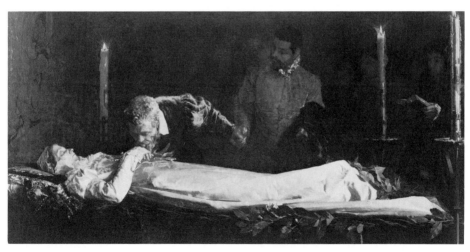

56 F. JACOVACCI (1838–1908), *Michelangelo kissing the dead Vittoria Colonna,* 1881
(Galleria Nazionale, Capodimonte)

57 M. Dicksee
(1858–1903), *Angelica
Kauffmann visiting Reynolds'
studio*, exh. RA 1892

58 German, 19th century,
Julius II visits Michelangelo

59 Waxwork, 20th century, *Primaticcio and Diane de Poiters*: detail (Musée de Cire, Chenonceaux)

female painter in his studio; since that period there had been no woman academician, and women altogether at the end of the 19th century felt their position difficult as far as the Academy was concerned.

But it is true that by that date depictions of past painters had largely ceased to have any significance. The great artist of the past might find himself lending lustre to some product in an advertisement, perhaps for what seems a German equivalent to Bovril.[69] And in our own day the 'history' picture has become a tableau, a waxwork one, as seen at Chenonceaux where Diane de Poitiers poses for Primaticcio.

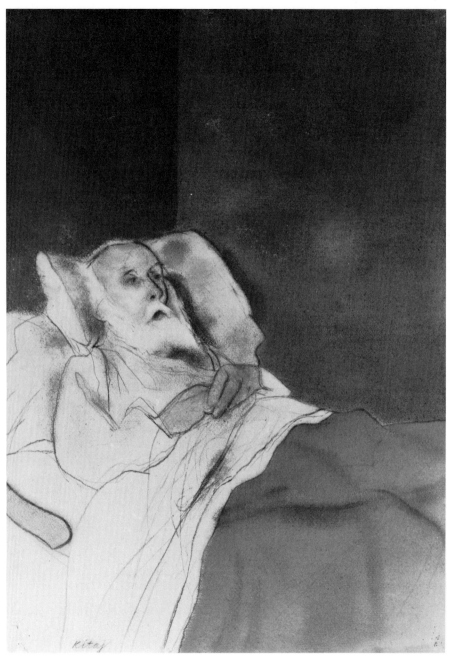

60 R. B. KITAJ (b. 1932), *Degas*, 1980

To end there would be too banal. And in fact, recalling the affinities of certain painters for past artists and the sense of belonging to a long tradition, we can find a moving example of very recent date, where without any anecdote homage is paid to greatness: Kitaj's pastel of Degas, grown blind and exhausted in the service of art.

Its message is that art matters, as we all tend to agree it does when we are gathered on a special occasion, rather as we might agree about the annual rite of Christmas pudding; we won't have to face it for another year. But the procession of images illustrated here is meant to play its part in emphasizing how deeply held by painters over the centuries has been the conviction that art is important. It seems fitting to leave virtually the last word to Degas, who crushed a minor fashionable painter for suggesting that painting is, after all, something of a luxury, with the retort: 'Yours is. Ours is a prime necessity.'[70]

It might be a better world if those of us who are not artists could at least subscribe to the prime necessity of art.

NOTES

1 The implications of the subject are vast; I do not attempt a bibliography but record some relevant work from which I have benefited: E. Kris and O. Kurz, *Die Legende vom Künstler*, 1934 and 1980 ed., with up-to-date bibliography; M. Winner, 'Zu Gustave Courbets Allégorie réelle und der Tradition', *Jahrbuch der Berliner Museen*, 1962, pp. 151–85; F. Haskell, 'The Old Masters in Nineteenth Century French Painting', *Art Quarterly*, 1971, I, pp. 55–85; and three exhibitions: *Maler und Modell*, Staatliche Kunsthalle, Baden-Baden, 1969; *Technique de la peinture: l'atelier* (Les dossiers du département des peintures, 12), Musée du Louvre, Paris, 1976; *Kunst – was ist das?*, Kunsthalle, Hamburg, 1977. I must also refer gratefully to the help I have had from colleagues at the National Gallery, especially Allan Braham, Christopher Brown, Dillian Gordon and Michael Wilson, bringing various examples to my attention. At an early stage Martin Royalton Kisch of the City Art Gallery, Manchester, kindly let me have a list he had compiled for his own research of pictures of artists by other artists. I am indebted also to David Rodgers, Curator of the Municipal Art Gallery, Wolverhampton, for providing me with a list of pictures dealing with old master subjects exhibited at the Royal Academy up to 1900 and for valuable advice on the whereabouts of several of them.

2 For the picture of Steen, see that by I. J. van Regemorter in the Rijksmuseum, repr. in *All the Paintings of the Rijksmuseum in Amsterdam*, 1976, p. 465. In 1828 Regemorter exhibited at the Royal Academy, London, a painting (no. 52) of Steen which has as sub-title the reference to Mieris and his wife.

3 De Keyser received international recognition and honours, special mentions at the Paris Salon and at least one English commission. Among other artists depicted by him were Rosa, Rubens, Titian and Memling.

4 Garnier sometimes took his subject-matter from Rabelais, and other piquant aspects are suggested by pictures of his with such titles as *Flagrant délit* and *Borgia s'amuse.*

5 Other later depictions of the impoverished painter range from Pieter Bloot to Rowlandson and Daumier; see the section on this aspect in the book accompanying the Hamburg exhibition, 1977, cited in Note 1.

6 Picasso's words are cited by John Richardson in reviewing the Picasso exhibition in New York, *New York Review of Books*, 17 July 1980, p. 24, where he writes of Picasso vainly pursuing immortality by painting himself into the company of Velazquez, Delacroix and Manet by his variations on their pictures.

7 For Titian's patent of nobility, see J. A. Crowe and G. B. Cavalcaselle, *Titian: his life and times*, 1877, I, p. 371.

8 Philip IV probably took this more literally than had the Emperor, but the link is increased since he was the Emperor's great-grandson and of course had inherited the pictures commissioned from Titian.

9 The fundamental study remains Dorothee Klein, *St Lukas als Maler der Maria*, 1933.

10 Mentioned by L. du Broc de Segauge, *Les Saints Patrons des Corporations*, n.d. but c. 1887, II, pp. 361–62.

11 A mid-14th-century example of St Luke painting the Crucifixion is illustrated in outline in Klein, op. cit., pl. VI, 3, repr. in the *Kunst – was ist das?* book, p. 98.

12 Klein, op. cit. pp. 13–15, for examples

drawn from Prague and Florence.

13 *Il Libro dell'arte*, ed. L. Magagnato, 1971, p. 5.

14 Further, see M. Davies, *Rogier van der Weyden*, 1972, pp. 204–5; for a likeness of Rogier, which does resemble the saint's face in the *St Luke*, Davies, op. cit., p. 38.

15 For these two pictures, further, see the catalogue of the exhibition, *Jean Gossaert dit Mabuse*, Rotterdam and Bruges, 1965, pp. 87–90, for the St Luke seated, and pp. 107–10 for the other composition. Additional literature on the theme is in the catalogue of the exhibition, *Le dossier d'un tableau: Saint Luc peignant la Vierge*, Musée de Rennes, 1974.

16 See S. Speth-Holterhoff, *Les Peintres Flamands de Cabinets d'Amateurs au XVIIe siècle*, 1957.

17 The subject discussed by F. Würtenberger, 'Das Maleratelier als Kultraum' in *Miscellanea Bibliotecae Herzianae*, 1961, pp. 502–13.

18 The version in the Louvre is catalogued, accurately enough, as *Le petit dessinateur*; that in the National Gallery has gone on being catalogued as *A Boy drawing*, which is not the same thing and misleading for what is depicted.

19 The box is very fully catalogued and discussed in N. MacLaren, *The Dutch School* (National Gallery Catalogues), 1960, pp. 192–95.

20 E.g. the comment in A. Blankert, *Vermeer of Delft*, 1978, p. 48, amid an otherwise very cogent discussion of the picture; the suggestion of a Burgundian element in the costume seems to originate with J. G. van Gelder, *De Schilderkunst van Jan Vermeer*, 1958, p. 14, along with the very confident statement, 'Die schilder is zeker niet Vermeer!'

21 This picture, a quite recent acquisition by the National Gallery, bears a damaged date, the last digit of which is missing entirely; it seems to read 166. Weenix was dead by 1663 at the latest.

22 An association with Leonardo's *Trattato* was first made by C. de Tolnay when discussing the picture in *Gazette des Beaux-Arts*, April 1953, p. 270.

23 For a recent thorough and careful discussion, with emphasis on the art of painting being honoured and the Apelles-Alexander theme reinterpreted, see J. Brown, *Images and Ideas in Seventeenth Century Spanish Painting*, 1978, pp. 87–110, an essay to which I am indebted.

24 That this plaster cast was owned by Fantin himself is pointed out by G. Weisberg in his article on the picture in *Gazette des Beaux-Arts*, Dec. 1977, pp. 212–13, reproducing a photograph of Fantin's studio.

25 Further see J. Pope-Hennessy, *Uccello*, 1950, pp. 154–56, for the picture's status and the identity of the artists in it.

26 Fitzwilliam Museum, Cambridge: *Catalogue of Paintings*, II, *Italian Schools*, J. W. Goodison and G. H. Robertson, 1967, pp. 147–48.

27 For Vasari's activity as an artist see P. Barocchi, *Vasari pittore*, 1964, and also T. S. R. Boase, *Giorgio Vasari. The Man and the Book*, 1979.

28 The decorations in Vasari's house discussed by W. Bombe in *Belvedere*, XIII, 1928, pp. 55–59; Boase, op. cit., pp. 183–85.

29 For a very full account of the ceremonies and the circumstances see R. and M. Wittkower, *The Divine Michelangelo, The Florentine Academy's homage on his death in 1564*, 1964.

30 A picture of the Bellini being taught by their father was exhibited in the Salon, in Paris, in 1845 (120) by L. M. J. Billardet: *Les Bellini*, with a long rubric (the original now at Besançon), and c.f. E. M. Ward's picture, exhibited at the Royal Academy in 1849 (303): *Benjamin West's first effort in art*.

31 R. and M. Wittkower, op. cit., pp. 106–7.

32 For the obsequies planned see C. Ridolfi, *Le Maraviglie*, ed. D. von Hadeln, I, 1914, pp. 211–18.

33 See *Le Opere di Giorgio Vasari*, ed. G. Milanesi, VIII (*Scritti Minori*), 1882, p. 528.

34 See H. Ost, 'Ein Ruhmesblatt für Raphael bei Maratti und Mengs', *Zeits-*

chrift für Kunstgeschichte, 1965, pp. 281–98.

35 Further for this frontispiece to *Galeriae Farnesianae Icones* (1686), see A. Pigler, 'Neid and Unwissenheit als Widersacher der Kunst' in *Acta Historiae Artium*, I, 1954, pp. 215–35, an article with a good deal of bearing on the present topic.

36 The subject was covered by an exhibition, *De Roem van Rubens*, Antwerp, 1977.

37 Referred to by C. Gould, *The Paintings of Correggio*, 1976, p. 156.

38 Discussed by M. Stuffmann in her article on La Fosse in *Gazette des Beaux-Arts*, July-August 1964, p. 109.

39 Further, for this, see B. Hercenberg, *Nicolas Vleughels*, 1975, pp. 157–58.

40 See the reprint by J. J. Guiffrey, 1872, of the relevant livret of the Académie de Saint Luc, 1752, nos. 50 and 51; the confusion is cleared up and corrected in an addendum; Eisen exhibited the picture again in the exhibition of 1762 (no. 16), the year in which his son Jean-Albert died.

41 A drawing of the subject by him is published by F. Irwin in an article dealing with 'Titian's first essay in colour,' in *Apollo*, Oct. 1978, pp. 251–55.

42 This was included in the exhibition, *Antonio Rafael Mengs*, Prado, Madrid, 1980 (no. 6).

43 Further, for this and other quite early and entertaining depictions of Rembrandt, see the article by R. W. Scheller, 'Rembrandt's reputatie van Houbraken tot Scheltema', in *Nederlands Kunsthistorisch Jaarboek*, 1961, pp. 81–118.

44 It is fully catalogued by N. Willk-Brocard, *François-Guillaume Ménageot*, 1976, pp. 65–67.

45 Attention is drawn to the treatments by Kauffmann and Cosway by R. Rosenblum, *Transformations in late Eighteenth Century Art*, 1967, p. 35, continuation of note 107, and see also note 108. Singleton showed his version at the Royal Academy, 1799 (no. 292).

46 Perhaps the next composition to be noted chronologically was 'The Death of Raphael', *dessin allégorique ... esquisse d'un*

tableau, exhibited by Guérin at the Salon of 1800 (no. 182); this is mentioned by R. Rosenblum, *Transformations in late Eighteenth Century Art*, 1967, p. 36, note 110, but through some lapse given to 'Harriet' (sic).

47 Among the many examples of art galleries decorated by reference to painters one might instance the Prado at Madrid, with statues at the two entrances of Velazquez and Goya, and the National Gallery in London, where the cornice around the dome area (Room 36) has busts of four British painters, Hogarth, Reynolds, Gainsborough and Turner, and four foreign ones: Michelangelo, Raphael, Titian and Rembrandt. In the adjoining rooms, barely noticed by most visitors, are relief decorations showing the studios of Phidias and Raphael. The work dates from 1876.

48 The subject treated by Charles Lucy and exhibited at the Royal Academy in 1863 (no. 44); Gainsborough was a much less popular choice, not surprisingly, for exhibits than Reynolds.

49 Painted by Delaroche and shown at the Salon in 1824 (now Musée Magnin, Dijon); see Haskell, loc. cit., fig. 21.

50 Painted by Wauters, and a good example of a painter who would probably not have been depicted had he not been afflicted in this way. The picture was very famous in its day; it was first shown at the Paris World Exhibition in 1878 (now in the Musée des Beaux-Arts, Brussels). Reproduced by Haskell, loc. cit., fig. 28.

51 For example, a picture of him sketching a ship, by H. E. Reijntjens, of 1884, exhibited in the very interesting exhibition, containing several other relevant works by different artists, *Het Vaderlandsch Gevoel*, Rijksmuseum, Amsterdam, 1978, (no. 52).

52 The point is made by Haskell, loc. cit., p. 67, discussing French attitudes, and seems broadly true for Europe altogether, though painters like Massys and Cranach, and even to some extent Dürer, are rediscoveries of the 19th century, make some appearances in pictures outside their

native lands and are not very likely to have been depicted very seriously much before around 1830. An early example of Massys is the picture by Richard Redgrave, R.A., 1839, (no. 377).

53 The Salon of 1817 was the first since the restoration of the Bourbons and was almost obsessively royalist; for the role of a critic at it, see H. O. Borowitz in *Gazette des Beaux-Arts,* Sept. 1980, pp. 63–74. For the theme of Poussin in 19th-century pictures, see R. Verdi in *Burlington Magazine*, Dec. 1969, pp. 741–50.

54 For Lawrence's reaction, including the disclaimer that he was another Titian, see D. E. Williams, *The Life and Correspondence of Sir Thomas Lawrence, Kt.,* 1831, II, p. 196.

55 E.g. the painting by Carl Jäger; further, for this, and the subject of the posthumous fame of Dürer, see the exhibition catalogue, *Dürers Gloria*, Berlin, 1971 fig. 40.

56 See the reference under note 3; according to Bénézit, *Dictionnaire des peintres, sculpteurs . . .*, 1976, 6, *ad vocem*, this picture is in the Stedelijk Museum, Amsterdam.

57 E.g. *Henry VIII and Holbein*, exhibited by Frederick Cowie, R.A., 1858 (no. 953); *Charles I receiving instruction in drawing from Rubens*, exhibited by Samuel West, R.A., 1842 (no. 267); *Philip IV of Spain knighting Velazquez*, exhibited by A. J. Herbert, R.A., 1856 (no. 286). An early picture by Millais of Van Dyck painting Charles I is in the Tate Gallery (T.G. 1808).

58 The picture, by Domenico Morelli, of 1851, is in the gallery at Capodimonte.

59 Other pictures by Leys dealt with Floris and also treated the theme of feasts of the Guild of St Luke.

60 That Guardi had had a difficult time selling his pictures, and sold them at much lower prices than those fetched by Canaletto's, represented probably the chief things known about him.

61 See the comment by R. Andree in the catalogue of the Kunstmuseum, Düsseldorf, *Die Gemälde des 19 Jahrhunderts*, 1968, p. 32.

62 M. Pointon, *William Dyce 1806–1864,* 1979, p. 6.

63 For comment on this aspect, see R. Rosenblum, *Ingres*, n.d. but 1967, pp. 98–99, reproducing some comparable treatments of Raphael in his studio.

64 Further, see M. Butlin and E. Joll, *The Paintings of J. M. W. Turner*, 1977, p. 123, citing J. Gage as demonstrating the autobiographical elements in the picture.

65 Butlin and Joll, op. cit., pp. 182–83, pointing out that this is the first (with a picture now lost) of Turner's oil paintings of Venice to be exhibited: R.A., 1833 (no. 109). It is interesting to note that in the same year Turner exhibited another 'old master' interpretation, *Van Goyen looking out for a subject* (no. 125).

66 It is treated amusingly by a highly unusual choice of subject, in a picture by N.-A. Taunay, dated 1824: *Francia being responsible for the installation of Raphael's S. Cecilia is overcome by the superiority of Raphael's work to his own*. This was in an anonymous sale, Christie's, 29 June 1979 (lot 38), brought to my attention by Michael Wilson.

67 O'Neil's picture was discussed at some length in *The Art Journal*, 1866, pp. 165–66, with a reminder that the painter had earlier treated the subject of the dying Mozart.

68 Painted by J.-N. Robert Fleury; reproduced by Haskell, loc. cit., fig. 9. It was also the subject of a now lost picture by Leighton, R.A., 1862 (no. 292): L. and R. Ormond, *Lord Leighton*, 1975, p. 154 (no. 80).

69 I owe my awareness of this to the book, *Kunst – was ist das?*, p. 114.

70 Conveniently cited in F. Sevin, 'Degas à travers les mots', *Gazette des Beaux-Arts*, July-August 1975, p. 37.

PHOTOGRAPHIC ACKNOWLEDGMENTS

Photographs have been supplied by the galleries and museums where the pictures are located, with the following exceptions:
Alinari 25, 30, 31; Courtesy Brooke Bond Liebig Ltd 58; Bulloz 21, 22; Giraudon 15, 23; Marlborough Fine Art (London) Ltd 60; Mas 5, 34, 38; Moro, Rome 47; Naples, Soprintendenza ai Beni Artistici e Storici 56; Pix 59; Scala 26; Courtesy of Sotheby Parke Bernet 1, 2.